C0-BIH-676

Cosmic Grooves:

Gemini

Cosmic Grooves:

Gemini

by Jane Hodges

CHRONICLE BOOKS
SAN FRANCISCO

Text copyright © 2001 Chronicle Books LLC
Executive Producer: Andrea Kinloch
Compilation Produced for Release: Dave Kapp, Mark Pinkus, and Andrea Kinloch
Remastering: Bob Fisher at Pacific Multimedia Corp.
Licensing: Wendi Cartwright
Project Assistance: Patrick Milligan, Amy Utstein, Mary Patton, and Mason Williams

Rhino Entertainment Company
10635 Santa Monica Blvd.
Los Angeles, California 90025
www.rhino.com

All rights reserved. No part of this book may be reproduced in any form
without written permission from the publisher.
Page 48 constitutes a continuation of the copyright page.

Library of Congress Cataloging-in-Publication Data available.

ISBN 0-8118-3063-2

Printed in China

Designed by Michael Mabry
Illustration copyright © 2001 Michael Mabry

Distributed in Canada by Raincoast Books
9050 Shaughnessy Street
Vancouver, British Columbia V6P 6E5

10 9 8 7 6 5 4 3 2 1

Chronicle Books LLC
85 Second Street
San Francisco, California 94105
www.chroniclebooks.com

Gemini
May 22 to June 21

Element: *Air*
Quality: *Mutable, a sign that adapts*
Motto: *"I think"*
Planetary Ruler: ☿ *Mercury, the messenger planet*
Mercury's Influence: *Mercury makes Geminis quick thinkers who are more influenced by their minds than by their hearts. Geminis live for change and mental stimulation and while they are a delight at a party, they require a lot of energy in more serious relationships. Geminis are usually lively and chatty, but also moody and changeable. Charm and articulate speech make them good companions.*
Symbol: *Twins*
Twins' Influence: *Highly rational Geminis are capable of holding two distinctly different viewpoints on the same matter, which makes them effective lawyers, journalists, psychotherapists, and academics. This duality, however, can make them feel detached from others' more single-minded approach. At worst, it depresses them; at best, it gives them great objectivity and insight.*

How to recognize a Gemini:
Rapid speech, hand gestures, darting gaze
Pick-up line: *"Read any good books lately?"*

What a Gemini wants:
Intellectual stimulation, variety
What a Gemini needs:
Introspection, focus
Jukebox selection: *"See-Saw"*

Introducing Gemini

Geminis are the zodiac's thinkers and curiosity-seekers. Ruled by cerebral Mercury ☿, Gemini folks are concerned with the power of the mind. Detached Geminis are driven by their desire to research, review, and explore new ideas. Though their curiosity often makes them quite outgoing and popular, they feel close to only a few people. Geminis like to keep social contact light and friendly, so they have easy access to and from others' lives and room to live unencumbered by needy friends. While they may seem detached, many consider them confidants—their candor and objectivity make them sage advisors on sensitive matters. Geminis sometimes change jobs, careers, and romantic partners abruptly, usually when they believe the possibility for learning has ended. However, if they can communicate their frustrations and remain committed, they will bring years of valuable input and connections into any relationship. Throughout their lives, Geminis are unpredictable. Their ideas move at lightning speed and their perceptions stimulate the people around them. Gemini children are precocious, witty, and articulate, but parents will need to find ways to prevent boredom.

A library card and advanced classes in school can help. Gemini teens may tend towards the rebellious, but are also accepting, curious, and great at rallying sports teams and organizing parties. As confirmed flirts, these youths may prefer to date many people rather than one. Gemini adults will need to keep dual careers, homes, or multiple hobbies to keep enough variety in life. Their partners will have to accept an ever-changing circle of friends and associates as well as adventure and debate. Gemini adults love and are loved by kids, because they understand the magic of discovery common both to children and to their sign.

In their spare time, Geminis love playing trivia games that jog their memories, and keeping up on current events and pop culture. They read every newspaper, magazine, and new book they can find, and enjoy crossword puzzles, word games, and poetry. Because the Gemini mind moves in two directions at once, these folks take easily to theater and to online forums, where they like the chance to create an electronic persona over e-mail or in chat rooms. Born communicators, they are skilled at organizing groups of people. Life, to a Gemini, is all about generating and exploring ideas.

Dedicated to Gemini

Twins like music that makes them think. These philosophers enjoy tunes that create a quirky or contemplative mood.

Chatty   Intellectual Geminis love to discuss lofty ideas, but *Talk Talk* by Talk Talk will remind them that actions speak louder than words.

Childlike   Known for mischief and charm, the adorable Peter Pan in every Gemini gets a theme song in *I Won't Grow Up* by The Fools.

Charming   The twins' gift of gab blends especially well with their impulse to flirt. In *Hanky Panky* performed by Tommy James & The Shondells we see where it all leads to.

Goofy   Twins poke fun at themselves as well as others. Their good-natured antics make for guaranteed entertainment, which is what The Coasters' rendition of *Charlie Brown* celebrates.

Stimulating   This sign's enthusiastic drive to find variety is applauded in *Live Wire* sung by Martha & The Vandellas.

Whimsical   Intellectual and quirky as adults, Geminis often start off as precocious children. *Playful Baby* by Wynonie Harris reveals just how smart Twin kids can be.

Flexible	Adept at making—and changing—plans on a whim, Geminis' adaptability and love of variety is what keeps them young at heart. In *I Ain't Particular*, Johnnie Taylor acknowledges their charming ability to go with the flow.
Complex	Born under the symbol of the Twins, this sign often has a conflicting yet dynamic understanding of the world, a perspective celebrated in *Gemini* by The Alan Parsons Project.
Indecisive	Commitment can sometimes be tough for Geminis, and *Mr. Duality* by The Bobs expresses this aspect of the two-minded Twin.
Lighthearted	Geminis like to keep things easygoing in any partnership, and *I'm Just a Kid* by Hall & Oates reminds the world that their light touch is a gift.
Unpredictable	In love and elsewhere in life, Geminis are anything but predictable, which is exactly what *See-Saw* sung by Aretha Franklin expresses.
Quixotic	From cerebral genius to spiritual sprite, the archetypes of the Gemini persona are mythologized in *Gemini* by Cannonball Adderley.

Gemini at Work

Born under an air sign, Geminis are idea people. They love collaborating and working with groups and are more motivated by mental stimulation than by getting paid the big bucks to do something mundane. The idea of not knowing what chaos the work week might hold excites them, so they thrive in a fast-paced environment where their instincts for multi-tasking and quick thinking get put to good use. At work, they surround themselves with stable personalities who counteract their flighty tendencies, a strategy that lets them play the role of visionary and idea person rather than the manager who cracks the whip. Their legendary charm can get them into and out of trouble quickly, for they can use the power of words to spin their colleagues in many directions. While they like to lead people—at least in terms of influencing their company's ideas—they can remain content in a supporting role when they have freedom to learn. Geminis like having access to information and power and working with the public. They love to get behind podiums, pulpits, and lecterns to motivate the masses.

Gemini Careers

Geminis are born communicators, researchers, and persuaders. Jobs where they must clearly articulate ideas and think on their feet appeal to them, so a career as a professor or doctor could be a good bet. Their outspoken nature makes them good critics, magazine editors, and local politicians. Geminis also make excellent researchers, journalists, producers, academic administrators, and even magicians. Publishing in all of its forms—of books, magazines, and Web sites—is a great profession for language-loving Geminis. Si Newhouse and Grace Mirabella succeeded in magazine publishing, while Nelson Doubleday and Alfred Knopf built their names in the book world. Since communicating in any form comes naturally to a Gemini, working with sign language or foreign languages appeals. Also adept with computer languages, many Geminis make successful computer programmers, systems administrators, multimedia designers, or video and animation artists. More detail-oriented Geminis may prefer to work as event planners, talent agents, or public relations professionals—jobs that give them variety and demand adept social skills.

Gemini in Love

Sociable Geminis value intelligence and open-mindedness in a partner and often need a mate as extroverted as they are. Men and women of this sign are fickle and changeable about everything, so their partners will have to be intellectually challenging and good-tempered to boot if they're to make it past the first dance with the unpredictable Gemini. These people can have prolonged sexual friendships without really committing, but to grow emotionally they need a partner who can simultaneously accept their changeability and notify them when it's time to get serious. Geminis secretly want to be disciplined and forgiven by their mates, but overt demands for structure and predictability make them balk. It takes a down-to-earth character to deal with the double-sided Gemini, but the relationship can be doubly rewarding when it works. Geminis share their entire public and private lives with loved ones. Mates who give them the freedom they need will be showered with Gemini humor, insights, and wit.

Gemini Relationships

Gemini & Aries (*March 21 to April 20*)		Passionate
Gemini & Taurus (*April 21 to May 21*)		Harmonious
Gemini & Gemini (*May 22 to June 21*)		Harmonious
Gemini & Cancer (*June 22 to July 22*)		Harmonious
Gemini & Leo (*July 23 to August 23*)		Passionate
Gemini & Virgo (*August 24 to September 22*)		Challenging
Gemini & Libra (*September 23 to October 23*)		Passionate
Gemini & Scorpio (*October 24 to November 22*)		Challenging
Gemini & Sagittarius (*November 23 to December 21*)		Passionate
Gemini & Capricorn (*December 22 to January 20*)		Challenging
Gemini & Aquarius (*January 21 to February 20*)		Passionate
Gemini & Pisces (*February 21 to March 20*)		Challenging

Miss Gemini and Her Men

Like Marilyn Monroe and Nicole Kidman, she can simultaneously seduce and challenge suitors with her flirty blend of smarts and sex appeal. She can also be the more approachable big-sister or best-friend type, like Helen Hunt or Brooke Shields. Either way, she wants a mate who gives her space for her full social and work life and who shares her sense of humor and enthusiasm. If he provides a grounding influence, it's even better.

Gemini Woman & Aries Man

Paula Abdul seeks Herbie Hancock.

This dashing man is one of the few people who can not only keep up with her, but also match her minute for minute with a frenetic, overbooked schedule packed with adventures, parties, and drama. Right from the start, these two will go places, and his spontaneity means he won't mind when she inevitably suggests a change of plans. After all, why go to the beach when there's a roller coaster to ride at the next highway exit? It's likely they'll meet at a party, since they both keep packed social calendars. The socially adept Miss Gemini may barely notice him at first, and he'll enjoy the challenge of getting her attention. She'll be intrigued by the creative way he comes on to her—and even more thrilled when they go behind closed doors. From first to last, these two busy characters will keep each other amused and intrigued. If she agrees to be his mate, she'll be saying yes to a life of adventure.

Gemini Woman & Taurus Man

Wynonna Judd seeks Willie Nelson.

His success appeals to her, but his love of routine is a drawback. He's one of the zodiac's great domestics, but she'll stay home with him only if she can play hostess to the constant parade of friends, family, and new acquaintances she likes to have around. The social cacophony may become the basis for compromise in their relationship. He'll rise to the occasion and help her co-host her parties. She'll decide she can be just as busy near the hearth as she was in her wilder party-going days. In the bedroom, Mr. Taurus's predictable style may bore her at first, but sexy Miss Gemini will coax him into new tricks. These two share a good sense of humor. In fact, Miss Gemini can even get him to laugh at his own stubborn streak—no small feat with this man. As long as she doesn't laugh at him when he's upset, this couple will share a friendly rapport that could ease into marriage.

Gemini Woman & Gemini Man

Lauryn Hill seeks Prince.

He's a professional juggler who balances women, work projects, and social calls simultaneously, so he understands that even the prospect of boredom sinks her into depression. Rather than judge the playful games she plays with other men, he appreciates her moxie. Rather than view him as a Peter Pan who can't decide what he wants to do when he grows up—not to mention whom he'll marry—she recognizes that he might be one of the few guys with the stamina she requires in a companion. They'll have to move in together after one date if they want to see each other since they both keep such a packed schedule. When they're not hosting parties, he'll whisk her off to the boudoir and whisper in luscious detail all the private things he'd like to do with her—things they'll then enact. When they marry they'll need a money manager, a personal trainer, and a really good alarm clock to keep them on track. They won't need any help keeping the sparks flying, though.

Gemini Woman & Cancer Man

Alanis Morissette seeks Ringo Starr.

This moody man has a complexity that fascinates her. One minute he's affable and goofy, the next minute he's needy and morose. She doesn't mind his mood swings, but she does mind when he chooses not to leave the house. He can be quite stubborn about remaining on familiar turf. They can work it out, though, if he'll drop his possessiveness and tidy the home and hearth while she flits about town. If she'll allow him to bring the dog or an old camera along on one of her adventures, he'll feel better. Back at home, he'll encourage her to snuggle up beside him and review the photo albums he's created of the journey, then seduce her into an adventure far better than any day at the mall. He'll teach her to turn her restless energy inward, and calm the nerves that drive her in so many directions. With work, they can create a restful partnership.

Gemini Woman & Leo Man

Stevie Nicks seeks Robert Plant.

He's even more popular than she is—which is really saying something. He knows everybody and insists only on the finest, while she's open-minded and insists only on variety. She's one of the few women who can get him to wait, which he'll remind her of when she slides into the seat next to him, looking like the million bucks he'd like to spend on her. His consistent warmth and generosity relax her active and restless mind. She has a hard time choosing which party to attend—after all, committing is not her specialty—but his voracious need to rub elbows with the rich and famous means he's already RSVP'd to ten events. She doesn't mind if he takes charge, because he's one of the few men capable of keeping her entertained. He'll see that it doesn't take a whole lot of finery to impress her—all it takes is being himself. His fiery sexual intensity appeals to her as much as her witty remarks challenge him. She'll decide it's not boring to be around someone focused after all—especially when he's focused on loving her.

Gemini Woman & Virgo Man

Gladys Knight seeks B.B. King.

This earnest man is as high-strung as she is. Because these two are both Mercury-led, they're ruled more by their thoughts than by their emotions. Once they start talking, though, there will be plenty of feeling expressed. Miss Gemini loves the way this brainy man has already finished the book she's reading, and Mr. Virgo is pleased to see this lady is as articulate and smart as he is. Sensitive Mr. Virgo may be shy about seducing her, but fortunately she's coy enough to find a way to lure him back to her place and let nature run its course. He'll listen attentively as she talks—and talks and talks—and try to offer her constructive advice. If she's careful not to laugh too hard at how seriously this earnest man evaluates the gossip that distracts her each day, and can find it in her heart to listen to his common sense once in a while, he could be a good match for her.

Gemini Woman & Libra Man

Nancy Sinatra seeks Jackson Browne.

He's easy to talk to, sociable, and capable of diplomatically handling her chaotic social life. As the zodiac's peacemaker, he's used to running the show in life and at work, but independent Miss Gemini won't let him take over her entire world. Unlike Mr. Libra, she doesn't want to wait around for the crowd to reach consensus. To keep up with her, he'll have to learn to get the show on the road and deal with the details later. This may make him nervous because he's used to making everyone happy, but the mistress of many moods will give him plenty of people to please—she is like an entire crowd packed into one lovely person. They'll feed off one another's sociability, and his tendency to see the world through rose-colored glasses will refresh her cynical viewpoint. At home, they'll share lots of laughs—especially about his sentimental streak, which she can't understand—and long sensual sessions in the bedroom.

Gemini Woman & Scorpio Man

Jewel seeks Adam Ant.

He's as intense as she is easygoing. The way he goes after what he wants makes her nervous, but it also makes her feel sexy. She may decide his intensity is somewhat compulsive, but because he always lays his cards on the table—a trait this straight-shooting woman appreciates—they can make things work if they compromise. He'll have to learn to loosen up and shed his suspicious nature. She'll have to tone down her social calendar. Physically, he will be a demanding lover who lavishes her with affection—and she'll realize he satisfies her every sexual whim. This relationship will work better if he makes sure the bills get paid, as Miss Gemini is as impulsive with money as Mr. Scorpio is intense with his emotions. He's open to her ever-changing mind, but demands a secure bank balance. If they stay together, she will lighten his brooding personality and he will convince this fickle lady to say "yes" to commitment.

Gemini Woman & Sagittarius Man

Suzy Quatro seeks Bruce Hornsby.

♂   ♀

She loves to learn as much as buff Mr. Sagittarius loves to travel. Unlike other women he's dated, outgoing Miss Gemini is game for any adventure he plans. Because neither of them wants to waste precious time planning, these flexible characters enjoy a shared spontaneity about life. She has a way of getting him to think about what he's doing, while Mr. Sagittarius has a way of getting her to pursue some of her eccentric but well-thought-out dreams. In bed, she need only say the word and Mr. Sagittarius will improvise to please her—and with great success. Neither one of them likes to stay in one place for long, so if they marry they will enjoy relocating to a far-flung continent, visiting friends in remote places, and logging frequent flier miles. They fulfill each other's wildest dreams.

Gemini Woman & Capricorn Man

Beverly Sills seeks Jimmy Buffet.

This serious man's success appeals to her. He's exactly the kind of man she likes—handsome, poised, diplomatic, and part of the "in" crowd. He exudes a quiet power and determination that's the exact opposite of her chatty, flirty social ways. However, his drive for security will ultimately clash with her need for variety and excitement. He doesn't like enormous changes at the last minute, which is just what makes her tick. When he makes a plan, he sticks with it. It will be easier to work out the kinks in this relationship if he gives her plenty of room and time for her own activities. As long as she gets home by the designated hour, he'll maintain his trust in her. In the bedroom, her casual style contrasts with his more calculated approach to making love, but if he's willing to put a little variety into their routine they'll enjoy one another. If these two rational creatures lay out the ground rules—and stick with them—this relationship could thrive.

Gemini Woman & Aquarius Man

Rosemary Clooney seeks Rick James.

These two recognize in one another a love of people. That Miss Gemini is two people in one is all the more appealing to Mr. Aquarius, who naturally understands this woman's detached multi-track mind. They'll talk late into the night unless they're enjoying their physical compatibility or tending to a friend in crisis. They'll change their minds ten times about what to do every day. The process of thinking through the possibilities may, for these two, provide more fun than the possibilities themselves. Their dynamic may sound wild and a little immature to some people, but this pair likes it. Variety is the spice of life—especially the love life of Miss Gemini and Mr. Aquarius. Both of these affable folks can create a strong friendship that serves as a foundation for their love. Each prizes a companion who is easygoing and flexible, as well as intellectual and exciting. This exuberant pair loves being together because they've both found a partner who sets them free.

Gemini Woman & Pisces Man

Laurie Anderson seeks Lou Reed.

Sociable Miss Gemini will find his wanderlust and detachment from his surroundings surprisingly familiar. Like her, he has an active imagination, only it inspires feelings and fantasies in him rather than eccentric but new ideas. She'll be able to accept his fickle moods, as she possesses them too. They often share a precise viewpoint and notice details no one else has ever noticed before. When Mr. Pisces realizes she understands his perspective on life, their mutual delight at finding creative soulmates in one another leads to their sharing a childlike enchantment about the world. They'll enjoy spending time together in artistic environments like museums, bookstores, and film festivals, where their imaginations can soar and collide. To make things work out in the real world—and in the bedroom—they'll have to compromise, as she can turn her feelings on and off more easily than this sensitive man. With a little nurturing from her and a little focus from him, they'll be able to bring magic to the home and hearth.

Mr. Gemini and His Women

*Brooding smart guys Clint Eastwood and Johnny Depp
are both Geminis, and so are affable comics
Gene Wilder and Andy Griffith. Whichever side of their
"twin" personality they choose to show, Gemini men
need a mate who gives them freedom to roam—but who can
also rein them back in when their imaginations and
curiosities start pulling them too far afield. The woman who
loves a Gemini will need to be a sociable and
ready traveler who won't get jealous when he strikes up a
chat with interesting strangers.*

Gemini Man & Aries Woman

Tom Jones seeks Lisa Stansfield.

This woman struts right into his life and takes charge of it. Fortunately, he likes the way she goes about this business. She's funny, feisty, naughty, and has as little respect for the status quo as he does. Like Mr. Gemini, she's a positive thinker. There's nothing she doesn't think she can do—and that includes taming his indecisive streak. He frequently changes his mind, jumping from one hobby or travel plan to the next. Fortunately, Miss Aries sees this habit as his decision not to follow through on an option rather than as broken promises. Where he forgets to follow through, she picks up the pieces. Soon they'll be running off to ski slopes and to parties and climbing mountains and racing triathlons. She's the one woman who can distract this distracted man—and he is one of the few men who can keep her from getting bored. They'll laugh their way to bed and continue giggling all the way to the altar.

Gemini Man & Taurus Woman

Boz Scaggs seeks Cher.

Miss Taurus can't help but draw a blank when she assesses his prospects as a long-term mate. Chances are he's not quite marriage material for this security-minded woman, but he makes her laugh so hard she'll remain open-minded. She's all about stability and commitment, and he's all about instability and freedom. If she gives him a long leash and doesn't nag him, he'll eventually settle down. No, he won't sit home by the fire every night, but he'll invite his friends over and throw a spontaneous party in the living room. He might even start to channel his energies into making the kind of money—especially if he's self-employed—that she needs to feel secure. In bed, she'll have to surprise him to keep his attention. Still, she's willing to work to preserve a relationship. If she can liven up their routine and if he can channel his energies close to home, these two will be happy.

Gemini Man & Gemini Woman

Hank Williams Jr. seeks Rosanne Cash.

She whirls in and out of his life faster than the Tasmanian Devil crosses the cartoon prairies, and the quicker she moves, the more he chases her. Watching these two is like watching two hummingbirds at a feeder—they hover so fast that others wonder how they remain airborne. This duo finds instant attraction in their constant motion. He can immediately sense where her mind is going before she even opens her mouth, and she loves that he understands her so well. She's one of the few women who doesn't raise her eyebrows when he abandons his latest hobby for the next new thing. Their days will be filled with hard-to-fathom conversations that only they understand and evenings of passionate drama—they both share a kinky inventive streak in the bedroom. They'll live surrounded by friends in a beehive of activity that, for them, creates inner peace.

Gemini Man & Cancer Woman

Morrissey seeks Debbie Harry.

The mother of the zodiac and the original Peter Pan might make a good couple. He admires her compassion—in fact, he wishes he had more of his own. She appreciates the way he takes time to look at life's ironies and quirks and, rather than focusing intently on one goal, lets his mind wander in creative tangents. While she won't like his free-spending ways, if he lets her take charge of the cash flow—or keeps her out of the loop so his habits won't unnerve her—they can sidestep the problematic money issue. Physically, they are compatible, but her moods can vary as often as his do. His idea of security is having someone who shares his love of learning and good conversation, and Miss Cancer has no problem keeping up with him. Her idea of security is to have a safe hearth and home and children running underfoot. With a little work, they can make a solid home filled with Crab comforts and Twins whimsy.

Gemini Man & Leo Woman

Curtis Mayfield seeks Jennifer Lopez.

She demands his attention the minute she walks in the room, and, for the sport of it all, he indulges her. They'll launch into a kind of primitive power struggle that, for them, serves as an elaborate foreplay. He'll quickly realize she's a true diva, and he's been chosen as one of her court jesters. He may try to resist—he doesn't clown around for other folks' entertainment, just his own—but he'll relent when she tosses him the sort of devastatingly coy come-on that he planned to use on her. She'll have him chasing her around, then he'll reverse the tables, then she'll be in charge again. As soon as they proclaim their love for one another things will smooth out, but the courtship might be so much fun that they prolong the chase. They shouldn't, for once they commit, they can really take each other places. His wild ideas spur her to action, and her wild behavior spurs more of his wild ideas. If they make it to the altar, they won't turn back.

Gemini Man & Virgo Woman

Cole Porter seeks LeAnn Rimes.

Creative Mr. Gemini finds it touching that she tries to bring order to his chaotic life. The fact that she respects his liberal ideas makes his heart beat even faster. Since cerebral Mercury rules them both, they use their minds wisely. However, while she uses her mind to organize and simplify, he enjoys ideas for ideas' sake and likes to inspire others creatively. The result is that he's constantly discovering new complexities, while she's always trying to eliminate the kind of chaos he enjoys. He'll get a kick out of her shocked response to his ideas and appreciate the polite—if predictable—way she tries to help him improve them. Miss Virgo makes an excellent, independent sidekick for the Gemini man who lives in his mind. However, she is shy and sensitive to criticism, which means he'll need to curb his blunt streak. In the bedroom, she is more sensual than cerebral, so Mr. Gemini will have to remember to check his chatter at the door. If they decide to commit, she'll be patient with his madcap ideas—and he'll realize thinking about a future with her could be the best idea he ever had.

35

Gemini Man & Libra Woman

Paul McCartney seeks Linda McCartney.

He sees through her girlish flirting and realizes that this smart woman needs someone who can fulfill her dual needs for companionship and fun. Still, she won't drop the pretenses of femininity just because he manages to make her laugh. She'll try and take charge of the relationship, and bring out her best negotiating skills to get him to agree with her about how they should spend their time. While she has a hard time coming to a conclusion, he is decisive—but keeps changing his decisions. As long as they agree to be together, they'll enjoy each other's company. They may not know what they're doing, or where they're going, but since they're both adaptable they have a great time exploring their options. He's funny, witty, charming, and has the most outrageous ideas. Miss Libra, always socially conscious, is a bit more diplomatic. Sexually, these two really know how to turn each other on—they both keep surprising one another in the most delightful ways. That's the dynamic that runs throughout this relationship, and if they keep the serendipity alive, their love will last.

Gemini Man & Scorpio Woman

Bob Dylan seeks Bonnie Raitt.

She exudes sexiness, and curious Mr. Gemini can't resist. She's not afraid of change, or of expressing her feelings, or of taking risks, so she's not afraid of him. This is the most daunting news of all, for when his legendary charm fails and he has to face her angry glare he'll realize he's met his match. This is one woman who'll insist he grow up. If he makes his best effort to be mature, tone down the flippancy, and come home on time, she'll reward him with warmth, compassion, and incredible fireworks in the bedroom. Yet just as they settle into a nice domestic routine, he'll up and say something silly during an intimate moment. If he's lucky, she'll believe he didn't really mean it, that he really is a grown-up. Because she's secretly one of the zodiac's most compassionate women, she'll almost always forgive him. They'll both do a lot of growing together. It won't be a bed of roses, but it will be an adventure neither will want to end.

Gemini Man & Sagittarius Woman

Boy George seeks Britney Spears.

Miss Sagittarius is married only to her freedom, and Mr. Gemini is married only to his mind. These two restless spirits realize that in each other they have an outlet for adventure. He's full of great ideas, and she's full of energy and pluck. While they are both hypocritical at times, growing defensive when they fall on the receiving end of the candor they often share with others, they are also both truth seekers in their own odd ways. If life is a journey, she's a friendly backpacker and he's a well-read tour guide. Her desire to explore the physical world and his desire to make verbal sense of it make them excellent companions. He can help her notice details she might ordinarily overlook, while she can lead him places he might not think to go. This dynamic carries over into their sex life—his ideas, and her creative enactments of them, bring them both much pleasure. They may decide, after a short time, that it's off to Vegas they go—straight to the honeymoon suite with the heart-shaped bed.

Gemini Man & Capricorn Woman

Miles Davis seeks Joan Baez.

She has a Mona Lisa smile, and he's determined to find out what's behind it. Meanwhile, she is as confused as he is—though this down-to-earth woman does her best to try and follow his logic, she'll somehow get lost in the avalanche of details he covers in a single breath. She'll find him unconventional, but get tongue-tied when he stops the monologue to ask her a direct question about herself. In fact, she may feel a shyness that she recognizes as the beginnings of a crush. He'll be somewhat disappointed that she turns out to be so practical, that the quiet look on her face is really just that—her sort of Zen way of handling life's problems and keeping control in a chaotic world. Sexually, he finds her mysterious and he may demand more variety during one evening of passion than she has experienced in a lifetime. They may not see eye to eye on anything, but he does know how to get her prim smile to widen into a grin. If she can make him laugh too, they have a shot at romance.

Gemini Man & Aquarius Woman

John Bonham seeks Sheryl Crow.

When she comes on to him in a foreign language and he responds in pig latin, they'll know it's time to party. These two extroverts love people and make a fantastic match. Watching them fall in love is like watching two best friends—and their huge circles of friends—get together. They'll have raucous parties, accompany one another everywhere, play Twister late into the night, run an ashram in their attic, and invite circus gypsies over for dinner. These two love to talk and will discuss everything, especially their pet liberal issues. Everyone loves their company. If they can get a moment alone, they will remember they make excellent lovers—they never cease to surprise one another. Their only argument will be over how big a wedding to have. Should they rent out Madison Square Garden or the Astrodome?

Gemini Man & Pisces Woman

Barry Manilow seeks Tracy Chapman.

Together they can imagine entire worlds in the course of five minutes, and create delightful artistic visions. They'll do well together if both of them are in the arts. She responds to things emotionally, translating her feelings into some creative medium. He responds to the world intellectually, with each new idea begetting dozens of new theories. While fantasy stokes their sex life, they'll have to work hard at creating a relationship that works well in reality. They love wandering through inspiring landscapes, museums, and poetry readings together, but neither one wants to handle the bill-paying and house-cleaning and cooking that characterize sharing a life. They'll both have to admit they need outside help to take care of the details neither of them wants to address. If they regard their relationship as a mystery, something of which they can know only halfway, they may find themselves in an exalted state that sustains them both for an entire lifetime.

Gemini at Home

The Gemini home is open and rambling. These people need space to roam freely. Because they love to be around company, Geminis do well with urban living, and a high-ceilinged downtown loft could be a good choice. As media maniacs, Geminis will have bookshelves in every room as well as all the latest electronic gadgetry and multiple phone lines. They don't like fussy or overstuffed Victorian styles, and their décor leans toward the modern. Twins tend to choose whites, lemon yellows, and light greens—colors that encourage clear thinking—as part of their color schemes. As long as there's enough space between the furniture to pace while they ponder, Geminis won't feel cluttered, even if the coffee table is stacked to overflowing with newspapers and magazines. Geminis are in nirvana with this stimulus nearby.

Gemini Health

The Gemini body tends to be slender and animated, and natives of this sign tend to move their hands around as they talk. Their disposition is generally positive and receptive, and Geminis are always happy to engage those around them in conversation. This sign rules the shoulders, arms, wrists, hands, brain, tongue, and bronchial tubes, which means Geminis are susceptible to bronchial infections, headaches, and tight arm and shoulder muscles. Because those born under the sign of the Twins gather—and give off—a lot of nervous energy, they need to learn how to relax and concentrate. By avoiding coffee and cigarettes, scheduling massage or yoga, and doing light exercise regularly, they can ward off the exhaustion their high-energy lifestyle creates. Geminis who want to quiet their churning minds can also benefit from meditation. With their slight builds and habit of eating small meals, they need not worry about their weight but would be wise to take preventative medicines and multi-vitamins throughout the year to ward off the flu.

Gemini Style

People born under the sign of the Twins have large wardrobes to accommodate all of life's social events. They like to shop but can have a hard time deciding what to buy, and tend to settle on basic styles that they can dress up or down with accessories even though their open-minded personality wouldn't mind wearing the wildest or latest styles. Geminis see having a large, versatile wardrobe as an extension of a full, versatile life. Gemini women are particularly adept at transforming their look and can go day-to-evening in a matter of minutes. During the workday, male and female Geminis wear conservative, tailored outfits, with the men opting for pastel shirts that bring out their sparkling eyes and the women using this sign's favorite color—pale yellow—for accent. Men born under the sign of the Twins will own beautiful watches and wear cufflinks or monogrammed sleeves. The women will wear fine rings and bracelets in stones such as green-gold beryl and keep their nails manicured.

On the Road with Gemini

These folks like lots of variety, so a road trip with plenty of stops along the way or weekend excursions throughout the year appeal to them. Gemini travelers want to learn from a vacation, and feel that the best way to accomplish this is to cover lots of turf and talk to natives. They'll do their research beforehand and then toss aside the tourist advice, preferring to explore the back-alley restaurants or rural country. The Eurailpass was tailor-made for Geminis, who enjoy the freedom to make spur-of-the-moment decisions. Geminis like visiting cities where they won't run out of things to do. They tend to choose liberal cities like San Francisco, where locals walk around doing their own thing. Party towns where fellow travelers are all game to meet one another, like Miami, Las Vegas, and Amsterdam, are other likely Gemini destinations. Because Geminis love to learn while they play, attending regional film, music, and literary festivals where they can soak up high art and local culture fascinates them.

Geminis are the best hosts in the zodiac and throw excellent cocktail parties. They love talking, mingling, and eating simultaneously and will serve up delicious and inventive appetizers in between introducing people to one another. They like to host theme parties that create a festive mood or celebrate events that call for guests to wear costumes. Offbeat holidays like Cinco de Mayo or Bastille Day give them the perfect excuse to learn how to cook with ten varieties of Mexican chile peppers or master the intricacies of French cuisine. Rather than get flustered by the preparations, Geminis are likely to invite a few friends over so everyone can chop and chat simultaneously. An expert organizer, the Gemini host gets into producer mode, assigning duties and encouraging all players in the production to do their part. The Twin host won't be content unless each guest leaves the party having made a new acquaintance.

In the Company of Gemini

Musicians:
Paula Abdul
Laurie Anderson
John Bonham
  (Led Zeppelin)
Rosanne Cash
Rosemary Clooney
Miles Davis
Bob Dylan
Boy George
Benny Goodman
Lauryn Hill
Jewel
Tom Jones
Wynonna Judd
Gladys Knight
Lenny Kravitz
Barry Manilow
Kathy Mattea
Curtis Mayfield
Paul McCartney
Alanis Morissette
Morrissey
Stevie Nicks
Cole Porter
Prince (The Artist)
Suzy Quatro
Boz Scaggs
Beverly Sills
Nancy Sinatra
Hank Williams Jr.

Peter Yarrow
  (Peter, Paul and Mary)

Performers:
Josephine Baker
Annette Bening
Sandra Bernhard
Drew Carey
Helena Bonham Carter
Joan Collins
Johnny Depp
Clint Eastwood
Joseph Fiennes
Michael J. Fox
Judy Garland
Andy Griffith
Anne Heche
Bob Hope
Helen Hunt
Angelina Jolie
Nicole Kidman
Jackie Mason
Marilyn Monroe
Liam Neeson
Joe Piscopo
Natalie Portman
Joan Rivers
Isabella Rossellini
Ally Sheedy
Brooke Shields
Jessica Tandy

Kathleen Turner
Mark Wahlberg
John Wayne
Dennis Weaver
Gene Wilder

Reformers:
Rachel Carson
Jacques Cousteau
Che Guevara
Rudolph Giuliani
John F. Kennedy
John Maynard Keynes
Henry Kissinger
Jean-Paul Sartre
Socrates
Dr. Ruth Westheimer

Artists:
Mary Cassatt
Isadora Duncan
Paul Gauguin
Egon Schiele
Kurt Schwitters
Frank Lloyd Wright

Athletes:
Lou Gehrig
Steffi Graf
Rocky Graziano
Vince Lombardi
Joe Montana
Joe Namath

Gale Sayers
Gene Tunney
Venus Williams

Writers:
Joseph Brodsky
John Cheever
Amy Clampitt
Ralph Waldo Emerson
Ken Follett
Anne Frank
Allen Ginsberg
Gail Godwin
Dashiell Hammett
Thomas Hardy
Jamaica Kincaid
Jerzy Kosinski
Robert Ludlum
Thomas Mann
Mary McCarthy
Colleen McCullough
Joyce Carol Oates
Sara Paretsky
Alexander Pope
Alexander Pushkin
Salman Rushdie
Marquis de Sade
William Styron
Walt Whitman
Tobias Wolff
W. B. Yeats

Permissions

Talk Talk
Talk Talk
(Ed Hollis/Mark Hollis)
℗ 1982 EMI America Records Inc., courtesy EMI Records,
under license from EMI-Capitol Music Special Markets.

I Won't Grow Up
The Fools
(Carolyn Leigh/Mark Charlap)
℗ 1980 EMI America Records Inc., courtesy EMI Records,
under license from EMI-Capitol Music Special Markets.

Hanky Panky
Tommy James & The Shondells
(Jeff Barry/Ellie Greenwich)
Controlled by Rhino Entertainment Company.

Charlie Brown
The Coasters
(Jerry Leiber/Mike Stoller)
Produced under license from Elektra Entertainment Group.

Live Wire
Martha & The Vandellas
(Brian Holland/Lamont Dozier/Eddie Holland)
Courtesy of Motown Record Company, L.P., courtesy of
Universal Music Special Markets, Inc.

Playful Baby
Wynonie Harris
(Wynonie Harris)
Courtesy of Delmark Records.

I Ain't Particular
Johnnie Taylor
(Isaac Hayes/David Porter)
Produced under license from Atlantic Recording Corp.

Gemini
The Alan Parsons Project
(Eric Woolfson/Alan Parsons)
℗ 1982 Arista Records, Inc., under license from
BMG Special Products.

Mr. Duality
The Bobs
(Richard Greene)
℗ 1993 Rounder Records Corp., courtesy of Rounder
Records Corp.

I'm Just a Kid (Don't Make Me Feel Like a Man)
Daryl Hall & John Oates
(John Oates)
℗ 1973 Atlantic Recording Corp., produced under license
from Atlantic Recording Corp.

See-Saw
Aretha Franklin
(Steve Cropper/Don Covay)
Produced under license from Atlantic Recording Corp.

Gemini
Cannonball Adderley featuring The Nat Adderley Sextet
(Nat Adderley/Walter Booker/Roy McCurdy/Rick Holmes)
℗ 1972 Capitol Records, Inc., under license from EMI-Capitol
Music Special Markets.

This Compilation ℗ 2001 Rhino Entertainment Company.